the stick book

loads of things you can make or do with a stick

jo schofield and fiona danks

For Connie, Dan, Edward, Hannah and Jake

© 2012 Quarto Publishing plc
Text and photographs © Jo Schofield and Fiona Danks 2012

First published in 2012 by Frances Lincoln,
an imprint of The Quarto Group,
The Old Brewery, 6 Blundell Street,
London N7 9BH, United Kingdom
www.QuartoKnows.com
www.goingwild.net

Jo Schofield and Fiona Danks have asserted their right to be
identified as the authors of this work in accordance with the
Copyright, Designs and Patents Act 1988 (UK).

A catalogue record for this book is available from the British
Library.

ISBN 978-0-7112-3241-9

Printed and bound in China

23

This book contains some potentially dangerous activities.
Please note that any reader or anyone in their charge taking
part in any of the activities described does so at their own
risk. Neither the author nor the publisher can accept any
legal responsibility for any harm, injury, damage, loss or
prosecution resulting from the use or misuse of the activities,
techniques, tools and advice in the book.
　It is illegal to carry out any of these activities on private
land without the owner's permission, and you should obey all
laws relating to the protection of land, property, plants and
animals.

MIX
Paper from
responsible sources
FSC
www.fsc.org   FSC® C016973

contents

discovering sticks

Let's go on an adventure. All you have to do is run outside and find a stick. Choose it with care and it can be anything you want it to be: a sword with which to fight off fierce dragons in the forest, a tracking stick to help you creep after secretive creatures, a wand to cast magic spells or a broomstick to transport you to other worlds.

The stick is perhaps the best-loved toy of all time, the starting point for endless adventures for generations of children all over the world. Sticks are easy to find, natural and, best of all, totally free. So, if you haven't got your own special stick, what are you waiting for?

The Stick Book is packed with activities to do with big sticks and little sticks, with dead sticks gathered from the ground and green sticks cut from living trees. Sticks are part of the natural world, providing food and shelter for birds and animals, so always collect them with care. In particular, cut green sticks very carefully so as not to damage trees.

While you can do a lot with sticks on their own, you can do even more by adding a few other simple materials.

Clay Wild clay can be collected from the banks of clean ditches and streams. (Alternatively, you can buy clay from educational suppliers or good toy shops.)

Natural paints To make natural paints you need a pestle and mortar and some water. Try making white from crushed chalk, brown or grey from clay mixed with water, black from crushed charcoal and red and purple from strained berries.

Stick adventure bag If you want to make the most of every trip outdoors, prepare a stick adventure bag, packed with:

- String, raffia, wool, thin wire and elastic bands
- Masking tape, double-sided sticky tape, PVA glue
- Old paintbrushes and sponges
- Scissors, secateurs and a sharp bushcraft knife, and small torches or night lights in jars (only include these if you are accompanied by a grown-up)
- A basic first aid kit

Wherever you are and whatever the weather, we hope *The Stick Book* will inspire you to get outdoors and discover the wonders of sticks and some of the secrets of the natural world.

With all the projects in this book, follow the safety guidelines on page 124. Some activities are easy to try and others are more challenging; remember that what is easy for one person may be tricky for another. The activity code below provides some guidance as to levels of difficulty and risk, but always take care when playing outdoors.

/ May be possible to do on your own

// Some tricky bits which might need a little adult help

/// Involves the use of tools (such as a knife), or fire, or being near water, so adult supervision is essential

1

adventure sticks

01

share the magic of a fire

NEVER make a fire without grown-ups present. Always follow the fire safety guidelines on page 124 .

● It's usually best to make your fire in a metal pan (a dustbin lid, hubcap or old wok), to keep it confined. Put the pan on rocks, wood or metal legs to avoid scorching the ground. If you make a fire on the ground, clear away leaf litter or cut out turf to give a base of bare soil.

● Collect tinder (dry fine material such as dried bracken or fluffy seeds) along with dead, dry twigs and sticks; this helps to get the fire going. Make a tepee of twigs as described below.

● The kindling tepee will eventually collapse. Let it form a hot bed of embers for cooking on or build it up again for warmth.

● Let the fire burn out. When it's completely cold, cover or remove the ash. Leave the site exactly as you found it.

Build a tepee of little twigs (kindling) over a bundle of tinder. Strike a match as close to the tinder as possible. When the tinder starts burning, add twigs, and then larger sticks as the fire builds.

cook over a fire

Cooking food above the fire instead of directly on the hot coals allows for more even distribution of heat.

Make a potholder Lash three sturdy, equal-length sticks together at one end, and then spread the other ends out over the fire. Hang a kettle, pot or griddle from a linked chain or a length of cord tied above the lashing.

Make a simple spit Push two forked sticks in the ground, one

on each side of the fire with the forks uppermost. Rest a sturdy straight stick in the forks above the fire for a spit.

Use a skewer Everybody loves toasting marshmallows over a fire, but how about cooking bread dough, meat or fish in the same way? Cut fresh straight sticks from a non-toxic tree or shrub – dogwood is ideal. Scrape the bark off and sharpen one end to a point to make a skewer. Thread sausages, fish, fruit or marshmallows on a skewer, or roll bread dough into a sausage shape to wind round it. Hold the skewer just above the hot coals, turning it occasionally so the food cooks evenly.

03

build a den

How about making a secret outdoor den? It could be a place to hide, play, have a picnic or spy on wildlife.

● Make a den in the back garden, a local park or in the woods. Choose somewhere with lots of sticks on the ground.

● Or try making a tepee: tie five or six long sticks together near one end. Stand them up vertically, with the tied end at the top, and then pull the poles outwards to form a tepee shape. Push the poles into the earth to secure in place and weave bendy branches (garden prunings are ideal) between the poles to make a lattice, filling any gaps with more leaves and branches.

Find a natural feature such as a large dead log or a low branch. Lean long sticks on this, binding them together at the top with stems such as blackberry runners, honeysuckle or wild clematis. Rest lots of smaller sticks close together along its length to make a wall. Cover this with a thatch of leaf litter.

make a diy tent

Going off camping? But don't have a tent? Try making a DIY tent from a large sheet of plastic, a rope and some long sticks. Or if you're going for a walk, take a tarpaulin so that you can have a sheltered picnic whatever the weather.

● Make your tent on dry level ground.

● Take two sticks, each about 2m/7ft long and sharpened at one end. Push the sharp ends into the ground about 2–3m/7–10ft apart, depending on the size of your tarp or plastic.

● To make the ridge use another stick or tie a rope tightly between the two poles. Attach two guy ropes from each pole; secure firmly in place with tent pegs whittled from sticks.

● Slide the tarp or plastic sheeting over the ridge until there is the same amount of material on each side. Tie short guy ropes along the sides, fixing them in place with pegs.

● This is just one design for a DIY tent; try experimenting with whatever sticks you have available and a tarp with built-in guy ropes.

05

make a stick sword

Perfect for woodland adventures! You can also make a cardboard sheath to carry your sword on your belt.

● Cut some green hazel to about 60cm/2ft long and another stick to about 15cm/6in.

● Hold the long stick where you want the handle to be and mark that point. To make the blade, angle a sharp, sturdy knife slightly towards the tip and make a 5mm/¼in cut at the marked point. Twist the knife upwards to split the stick, and then run it down the stick to remove a whole strip of wood. Repeat on the other side.

● Whittle each side a little more to make a flat blade, and then round off the tip for safety.

● Place the smaller stick (the handle) upright on a firm surface. Ask someone to hold the knife blade on the end of the stick; hit the knife blade with another stick until the handle stick splits into two equal pieces. Place these pieces round the sword at the top of the blade and bind together tightly with string.

06

make a catapult

Stick catapults are great for firing soft ammunition such as berries or flour bombs, but make sure everyone is wearing goggles and old clothes. Never aim catapults at animals.

● You will need some stretchy material, or better still catapult elastic, which is a available by the metre from internet suppliers.

● Select a living symmetrical Y-shaped stick. Ask a grown-up to help you cut it about 20cm/8in below the fork, using a saw or loppers, at an angle so that water can drain from the stump.

● Cut the Y-shaped stick to the size you wish. Scrape the bark off with a knife, making the wood as smooth as you can.

● Carefully cut a notch at the top of each arm of the fork.

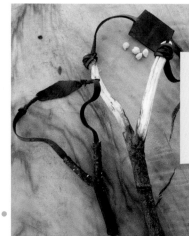

Cut the catapult elastic or stretchy material to about 60cm/2ft and then twist it tightly around the notches and secure with a knot.

make a pea-shooter

The soft pith inside a young stem of elder can be hollowed out to make a tube, ideal for a pea-shooter.

● Sharpen one end of a hard stick with the same width as the elder's soft pithy core. Use this to bore the pith out of the elder stem. Work from both ends; the longer the pea-shooter the harder this is, as the pith gets compacted in the middle. If you are at home, try using a kitchen skewer and adding a little water to soften the pith.

● Peel the bark off the ends of the pea-shooter.

● Personalize your pea-shooter by scratching patterns into the surface with a nail, rubbing berry juice or charcoal into the scratches and then sanding it down. Alternatively, use a pyrograph tool to burn patterns into the wood.

21

08

make a bow and arrows

How about having your own made-to-measure bow to bring outdoor adventures alive? Or try making a tiny one for a woodland elf.

● Cut a bendy stick to the required length, adjusting it to your size. Shorter bows perform well and are easier and safer to use.

● Carve notches about 2cm/¾in from each end. Attach string around one notch using a slipknot. Pull the string tight so that the bow forms a wide arc. Wrap the loose end of string round the other notch and secure it with a strong knot such as a couple of half-hitches. Ensure the knots are tight so that the bow does not spring out of position. Make sure you can feel tension in the bow as you pull the string back slightly.

For arrows, collect thin straight sticks from the woodland floor or cut slender lengths of green hazel or willow. Once you have fired your arrows, make sure everyone lays down their bows before collecting the arrows. Leave safety instructions for your elf!

make a staff

With a little imagination any old stick can be transformed into an imaginary weapon to liven up outdoor adventures.

Long straight sturdy sticks make great staffs; hold at each end and challenge your friends to a battle! Try balancing on a fallen log; can you and a friend use the staffs to try and knock each other off the log? Be careful not to poke a stick near anyone's eyes or bash them too hard.

Perhaps a staff can make you into a powerful wizard or a fearless explorer.

10

make a spear thrower

The atlatl (pronounced 'atal-atal') is the best way to throw a stick spear.

● Find a straight forked branch with a diameter of about 1.5cm/½in and cut just below the fork; the main length should be about 50cm/20in. Cut the other side off, leaving a short spur of about 2cm/¾in at an angle of about forty degrees to the main shaft, and in the same plane. Cut the spur to a point.

● Make a spear from a straight stick of light, flexible wood. Carve one end to a point and make a small notch in the other end. Add flights made from feathers or plastic (e.g. from a milk container).

Put the atlatl's spur into the end of the spear. Hold them side by side in your throwing hand, as illustrated. Place your hand by your shoulder, and hold the spear in place with forefinger and thumb. It should be in line with your eyes.

● Make a target in an open space, such as some balloons in a tree or a circle of sticks on the ground.

● Release as if throwing a cricket ball: swing back a little and then throw at the target. At the point of release do a fast hammer-like motion downwards with the atlatl.

Warning: Atlatls are potentially dangerous weapons; never use them to throw spears at people or animals. Make sure everyone stands well behind anyone using the atlatls. Wait until everyone has had their turn before retrieving the spears.

magic sticks

make a star wand

These wands only work their magic outdoors; don't forget to practise your spells before using them!

● You need a freshly cut thin bendy stick – any sort of willow is perfect – at least 1m/3ft long.

● Make a fold about one-third of the way from the stick's thickest end. Make three more folds, each about 5–10cm/2–4in apart.

● Straighten the stick, and then bend it at the lowest two folds to make a triangle like a back-to-front 4. Feed the stick tip right through the triangle, teasing it through gently until you have made two points of a star.

● Loop the tip of the stick round behind the right-hand edge of the triangle and back through to make a star.

● Wind the thin end of the stick down the wand's handle, and tie a knot to secure. Decorate as you wish.

12

/// make a wizard's wand

Just imagine having a wand like Harry Potter, to get you out of all sorts of tricky situations!

● Find a magical stick – or better still, let it find you.

● Use a knife to scrape off all the bark, or to make patterns. Sand the wood to make it smooth if you wish.

● Carefully whittle the tip of your wand into a point. Varnishing or painting with diluted PVA will make the wand last longer.

make a wiggly snake

This wiggly-stick snake is made from an elder stick and a ribbon.

● Cut the stick into 2.5cm/1in lengths. Carefully split each one in half lengthways using a knife.

● Glue one half of each length on to one side of a ribbon and the other half on to the other side.

● Use a thicker piece of elder as the snake's head, and add a leaf tongue. Decorate with chalk and other natural paints.

● Tie another stick to the snake's head with cotton. To make the snake wiggle, hold its tail and move the stick.

14

make scavenging sticks

Some fun ways to collect interesting natural treasures.

A story stick Attach loose natural materials to a special stick with coloured wools, elastic bands or double-sided tape. Use your stick to help tell a story. How about a detective story? Why didn't the squirrel finish his nut? Who lost that feather and why?

An aboriginal journey stick Decorate a stick to remind you of a journey to the woods or park or to remember a special wild place you'd like to go back to. Use coloured wools to represent natural colours and add natural materials you find on the way, such as grasses, long leaves, seeds and feathers.

A shaman's stick Shamans are mystical characters who live in wild places. Make a shaman's stick for imaginary games in which you wander between different worlds. Decorate it with natural colours painted on in wild patterns; bells (to clear the air); feathers (birds represent the shaman's spirit flight); bones (they have the power the channel the spirit) – use only clean bones bleached by the sun, such as a rabbit's skull or leg bone; .

A rainbow stick Wind double-sided tape around a stick. Collect tiny pieces of colour, such as leaves, blades of grass, petals or seeds and stick these along the tape to make a rainbow effect.

make a witch's broomstick

Do you fancy sweeping the yard? Probably not; but how about a game of quidditch? Or a Hallowe'en adventure?

● Choose a sturdy stick; if you plan to fly long distances, make sure it is strong and has a comfy place to sit!

● Collect some twiggy stuff such as birch twigs or the woody stems of marjoram or lavender. Gather these in a bundle around one end of the stick and tie securely with string, raffia, bramble runners or clematis stems.

● Tie on another layer of bristles a little above the first layer and repeat until you have a nice bushy broom.

16

make stick characters

Look for the most twisted, gnarled stick you can find. Could it become a little man, a scary troll or a magical sprite?

● Mould a ball of clay (see page 6) into a weird and wonderful face. What natural things can you find to make crazy hair, staring eyes, fierce teeth or sticky-out ears?

● Use raffia or masking tape to fix on arms and legs. Make clothes from grasses or leaves and decorate with natural paints.

● Or try making simple marotte puppets, rather like a jester's stick. How fierce or friendly can you make yours?

Can you find a place to hide your characters? This fierce troll is guarding a bridge.

make stick and clay animals

● Mould clay into the shape of an animal, an imaginary monster or even Rudolf the red-nosed reindeer. Use sticks and twigs, paints and other natural materials to add legs, antlers, horns or prickles.

● Let your imagination run wild. There are lots more ideas on the following page..

18

make a fairy house or an elf castle

Have you ever made miniature houses for fairies or elves? Try making them in the woods, at the beach or at the bottom of the garden, using sticks, stones and other loose natural materials. And, who knows, perhaps a real fairy might move in!

● Find a good spot – perhaps among tree roots, in a hollow stump, in a pile of stones or in a dip in the ground.

● Search for loose natural materials such as bracken, twigs, moss, hazelnuts, beech mast, fir cones, acorns, or whatever you can find.

● Use these to make an elf house or castle, or have a go at making fairyland details such as a table laid for a woodland feast, armour and weapons for an elf or a mermaid's seaweed costume.

make tiny worlds for toy people and animals

How about taking your toy soldiers or farm animals out for an adventure?

Perhaps the soldiers would like a stick fort in the woods, or the animals would like a farm or a zoo at the bottom of the garden. Make them a miniature world in which the toys are the only non-natural things.

make hobby animals

Dig out the odd sock collection and try making a hobby deer, a seahorse, a unicorn or a dragon.

● Stuff a sock with scrunched-up newspaper or straw. Choose an animal to make (this might depend on the colour of the sock) and then mould the stuffed sock to the right head shape.

● Push a long sturdy stick into the sock and tie the end of the sock to the stick.

● Use double-sided tape to attach seed eyes, leafy ears and a twig mouth to bring your animal to life. You could add twig antlers or a stick horn or tusk.

● Explore the woods on your hobby animal.

make woodland monsters

If you look very carefully you might find all sorts of weird and wonderful monsters lurking in the woods. Can you bring them to life?

● Look for interesting shapes in tree trunks, branches, tree stumps or fallen logs. Perhaps a knot in the bark might be an eye, a broken branch might be a snout or a curving branch might be the body of a snake.

● Can you see a tree with a face – like an Ent from *Lord of the Rings* – and an old tree man smoking a pipe?

● How about making crazy characters from old tree stumps or branches, like this mad professor complete with stick hair and wool moustache?

● Or make a clay head, find a place to put it, and then add stick hair and seed eyes to make a crazy monster.

22

make woodland magic carpets

Imagine flying off to some faraway land on your own magic carpet! Design magic carpets in the woods or the park on an autumn day.

● In a woodland clearing use sticks to make a frame.

● Fill the frame with a pattern or picture made from coloured leaves, seeds, berries and sticks. Or make smaller frames so that each person can design their own section of the carpet.

● Get everyone to stand on the carpet and make up a story about flying off to discover an enchanted kingdom.

See who can make a woodland magic carpet with the wildest or most beautiful design.

making a flying creature

Can you use sticks to make the shape of a giant butterfly or an exotic bird on the ground? It may look rather drab, so bring it to life by colouring it with patterns of leaves. Lie down and become the creature's body, relax as you look up at the clouds or the leaf canopy and dream of flying away . . .

24

make fairy or fish sticks

Transform bendy willow sticks into magical springy wands for fairies or bouncy toy fishing rods.

● Weave green willow into fish or fairies, adding more willow or creeper stems to decorate.

● Wrap brightly coloured fabric or felting wool round a bendy stick. Wind knitting wool over the top to secure it in place.

● Tie your willow fish or fairy to the end of the stick, and then go off outdoors for some bouncy adventures.

make wild storyboards

This game is for two or more teams. Each team thinks of a well-known story set in the natural world.

● Each team makes a storyboard out of sticks by making a row of three or four similar-sized frames on the ground. Using loose natural materials, each team tells their story in a series of two- or three-dimensional pictures in the frames.

● Everyone tries to guess the stories the pictures are illustrating. Do you recognize *The Very Hungry Caterpillar* in the picture below?

3

creative sticks

26

make a picture frame

Picture frames help us focus on a distant view or on something near by. Make one from a bendy stick, or find a spy hole in a rotting branch – what can you see? Or decorate a stick frame to remind you of a special place.

● Lash four interesting sticks together to make a frame. Twist creeper stems around it and then decorate it with natural materials, poking them between the creeper stems and sticks.

● You could use the frame around a photo or a collage of your special place, or weave things across it (see page 65).

27 make a paintbrush

Remove bark from a straight stick of elder. Cut a feather to about 7cm/3in, and push it into the stick's soft pith. Use the brush to paint with watercolours or natural paints (see page 6).

make a woody crown

What can you find to decorate a crown fit for a woodland fairy or forest king?

● Bend green willow into a circle to fit your head; continue weaving the ends around until they are completely woven in and the circle is quite secure.

● Twist a length of ivy, clematis stem or raffia around the crown base and then decorate with seasonal natural materials.

make charcoal pencils

Place one end of a stick in the embers of a fire for a few minutes, and then let it cool down. Use the blackened end to draw on rocks or paper. Only draw in places that will be washed off by the tide or the rain; leave no trace.

30

create stick art for a woodland gallery

Try creating a natural art gallery in the woods for your friends to discover; it could be part of a magical trail or perhaps something for other people to add to.

● Crown your favourite tree the king of the forest! Arrange sticks round the tree, and decorate the crown with other natural materials if you wish.

● What other natural sculptures can you make with sticks, mud and whatever else you can find in the woods?

Make mud balls round a stick, and cover them in moss or other natural materials.

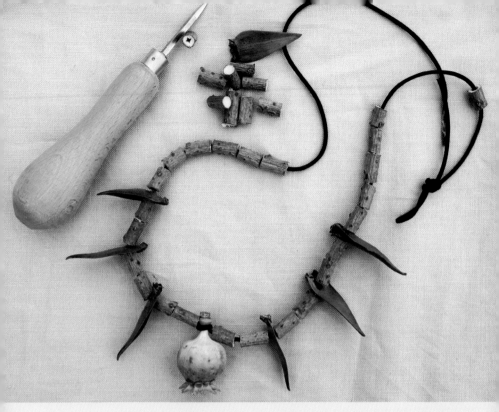

make a necklace

Yes, it really is possible to make a necklace out of a stick!

● Cut an elder stick into about twenty-five 1cm/½in lengths. Hollow out each piece with a bradawl or skewer.

● Paint the beads with natural paints and coat in diluted PVA for a better finish.

● Thread the beads on a cord to make a necklace or bracelet. Tie knots or add seeds, leaves or feathers between the beads.

draw in mud and sand

Write or draw patterns and pictures with a stick in squidgy mud or firm sand. Or dip a stick into thick mud and draw on a rock, a leaf or a tree trunk.

Can you find a special stick to mix and mash natural materials into sweet scented perfumes?

choose a stirring stick

A special stirring stick is just what you need to make magic potions, smelly cocktails or petal perfume.

Cocktails and perfume Pour a little water into a clear plastic cup and add fallen petals, natural herbs, pretty leaves or wild fruits. Whose concoction smells the best?

Potions Collect weird and wonderful natural things – perhaps a pinch of fairy dust, and a drop of dew from a spider's web or some slime from a slug's trail. Use a crooked stick to mix a magic potion and then cast a spell on your friends!

34

make a nest

This could be a tiny nest for a bird or a huge one for you or even for a dinosaur. Can you find anything to use as eggs?

● Collect sticks, grasses, mud and perhaps moss, lichen, feathers, fluffy seed heads and sheep's wool. Weave the sticks to make the base of a nest and then line it with softer materials. Put the nest somewhere protected and safe from predators, such as in a hedgerow or wall.

● At Easter time make several nests and hide them around the garden. Perhaps the Easter Bunny will fill them with eggs . . .

How many nests can you find around the garden filled with chocolate eggs?

make a dream-catcher

Native Americans believed that webs of natural fibres trapped bad dreams, only allowing the good dreams past. Have a go at making a dream-catcher to hang near your bed.

● Bend a freshly cut stick into a small circle (see page 57).

● Attach a long piece of thread to a point on the circle, pull it to the opposite side of the circle and wind it around the stick a couple of times. Repeat several times to make a web.

● Take the dream catcher out on a walk. Weave natural materials through it and hang shells and feathers from the bottom.

make a loom for wild weaving

Forked stick loom Tie raffia, string or wool to the base of a forked stick and wind it up and round. Take the loom outside with you and find natural materials to weave through it.

Straight stick loom Lash four sticks together in a square, and then tie a couple more sticks across to split the square into three rectangles. Looking for different textures and colours, collect bundles of grasses, coloured stems, ivy, sheep's wool or feathers to weave between the sticks. Tie on other materials such as cones if you wish.

Straight stick loom
Visit a special place in spring, summer and autumn to weave seasonal pictures.

37

wild weaving

Have a go at some wild basket-making. Use secateurs to cut the sticks.

● Make a 1m/3ft length of green willow into a ring (see page 57).

● Cut about thirty sticks, each one at least 5cm/2in longer than the diameter of the circle. Fix one stick across the circle.

● Weave the other sticks in the opposite direction to the first stick, until you have filled in the circle.

● Cut off the ends of each stick so that they are flush with the edge of the circle. If using fresh willow, let the sticks dry before cutting them, to allow for shrinkage.

decorate a stick tree
with stick stars

In spring put living sticks in a vase of water and watch the buds open. In winter arrange dead sticks in dry Oasis or pebbles in a jar. Decorate your stick trees with blown eggs for Easter, pressed flowers for midsummer, coloured leaves for Hallowe'en, berry baubles, advent leaves, chocolate and stick stars for Christmas.

Stick stars Bend a stick in four places to create five equal lengths and then follow the instructions for making a star on page 31. Tie the loose ends together with fine wire. Decorate the stars with chalk paint, or silver or gold spray, or twist a coloured ribbon or a length of ivy around them.

39

////

make stick and paper lanterns

Who needs a torch after dark when you can enjoy a woodland walk or a picnic lit by magical stick lanterns?

● To make the base, cut sticks to the length you require for whatever shape you wish – circle, square or triangle – and fix together with masking tape. Don't make the lanterns too big; smaller ones are much easier to make. Tape a small jar or a torch on to the base.

● Build the frame up to make the shape. Make a loop at the top so that the lantern can be hung up or carried on a stick.

● Cover the frame in wet-strength coloured tissue paper (see page 125), sticking it with masking tape or by coating the frame in PVA glue. To decorate the lantern either paint the tissue paper or stick on tissue shapes.

● Sponge the lantern with diluted PVA to make it stronger. Leave to dry.

● Make sure the base is open so that the night light or torch can be inserted into the jar. Cut a small hole at the top of the lantern to let the heat out.

● For more instant lanterns, cut shapes in a paper bag with handles. Place a small torch in each bag, and then string the lanterns on sticks for a lantern procession.

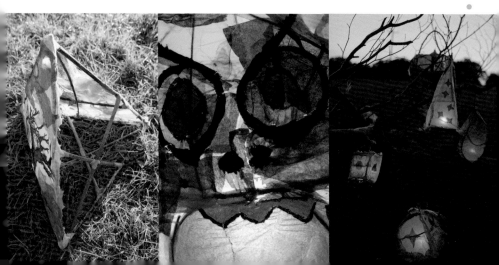

40

make natural mobiles and wind chimes

Try making natural mobiles and wind chimes to celebrate any occasion – Christmas, Diwali, Valentine's Day, midsummer . . . Hang them among trees or outside a window, where they can move and tinkle in the breeze.

● **Easter mobile** Weave willow rings (see page 57) and join them with fine wire to make an egg shape. Make a moss-lined nest (see page 62) to place in one ring. Decorate with blown eggs, feathers and seasonal flowers.

● **Autumn mobile** Choose some natural autumn treasures and use a bradawl to make holes through any seeds and nuts. Thread the treasures on wool and hang them along a stick. You could make little characters such as a flying pig or an insect, or thread berries along a wire to make a ring or a spiral.

● **Make a wind chime** Search for loose natural materials that make a sound, such as broken shells, pebbles or hard seeds, and also manmade materials such as old buttons or bits of scrap metal (ring pulls, can lids, nails). Tie these along a stick, making sure they are close enough to knock together.

41

make a wreath

A natural wreath welcomes people to your door at any time of year or cheers up a table as a centrepiece.

- Twist bendy willow or hazel sticks into a ring (see page 57). Add more sticks to build up a thicker ring, twisting them round as much as you can until the whole thing holds together.

- Thread stems of leaves through the woven willow and tie other natural decorations in with wire if necessary.

- Decorate with brightly coloured leaves and fruits for Harvest Festival, eggs and yellow flowers for Easter, orange seeds for Hallowe'en, and, of course, berries and greenery for Christmas.

- This basic stick wreath can be used over and over again.

4

stick games

42

play pick-up sticks

A DIY outdoor version of the traditional game.

● You need about forty reasonably straight sticks all of a similar length.

● Use natural chalk paint (see page 6) to paint one, two or three lines around each stick to show how many points each stick is worth.

● Hold the sticks in an upright bundle on level ground and let them fall randomly to the ground in all directions. The first player tries to remove one stick without moving any other sticks. If the attempt is successful he or she keeps that stick and has another turn; if unsuccessful, it is the next person's turn.

When all the sticks have been picked up, add up your points. The player with the most is the winner.

throw a stick for a dog

Playing with a stick makes a walk more fun for everyone, not just the dog! But help your dog choose a stick without sharp edges and watch out for a dog trying to grab your hand rather than the stick by mistake.

44

make a flying machine

On a windy day, try transforming a pile of sticks, paper, sticky tape and card into flying machines.

Go to an open hillside or field (make sure it's not near a road) for a flying competition. Whose plane can fly highest and furthest? Who can come up with the most impressive or the wackiest design?

● Tape two straight sticks together in a cross: one for the body of your machine and the other for the front edge of the wings.

● The rest of the design is up to you, but here are a few tips. Make wings from a plastic bag, paper, garden fleece or some other lightweight material. They must be large enough to lift the plane into the air. Stick them in place with a small amount of tape. Cut out tail flights from thin cardboard or a plastic milk container. Stick a small weight (e.g. clay, a small pebble, an old nail) on the machine's nose.

45

play capture the flag

This game for two teams is an all-time favourite – you just need some sticks and a large outdoor space.

● Make two flags by attaching long strips of fabric (or bandanas, T-shirts or even big leaves) to sturdy sticks.

● Each team needs a territory. if there is no obvious boundary, mark one with sticks. Have one area within each territory as a jail.

● Each team puts their flag in their own territory, in a spot visible to the other team. The aim is to steal the other team's flag and place it in your own team's territory without being tagged.

● Anyone caught by a member of the other team is out of the game or goes to jail until released by one of their own team.

● If someone steals the flag but is tagged while running back to their home territory, the flag must be returned to base.

play aunt sally

You will need six throwing sticks, about 45cm/18in long and 5cm/2in in diameter, and a ball, stone or chunk of wood to use as a skittle (called a dolly).

● Play this in an open space, so nothing can be damaged by flying sticks. The dolly should be about 75cm/30in above ground level, so place it on a wooden post or something heavy, such as a metal outdoor umbrella stand.

● Lay a long stick on the ground about 10m/30ft from the dolly; each player stands here when playing. Reduce this distance if it's too far.

● Decide how many rounds to play. Sticks must be thrown underarm and each player gets six throws per round. The person who hits the dolly off the post the most times is the winner.

invent stick games

How about using sticks to invent your own new games? They could be for two people or a crowd, for mixed age groups and to suit the space and the environment. Try to avoid arguments by fixing the rules before you start.

stick tower challenge

Who can build the tallest free-standing stick tower in just twenty minutes?

The challenge is for each team to work together and build a tower using twenty straight 60cm/2ft sticks and a ball of string.

● For an extra challenge, each tower must stand up for five minutes to qualify for the competition.

play quoits

A stick version of this traditional game.

● Push a sharpened stick (the pin) into the ground. Lay four 50cm/20in willow sticks in a square around the pin.

● Make four quoits by twisting bendy sticks into circles (see page 57). Mark the playing position with a long stick.

● Each player throws four quoits in a round. Throwing a quoit over the pin scores two points or within the square scores one point. The first person to get to twenty-one points is the winner.

50

play tracking with sticks

Lay a trail of stick arrows through the woods or park and see if your friends can find you. This is a group game: everyone must team up with at least one other person and stay together at all times.

● Agree on a trail code, which could include the following: **cross**: a dead end, a false trail; **two arrows with a stick in between**: the trackers should go over an obstacle in the path (such as a fallen tree); **arrow with two arrowheads**: the party has split up; **arrow alongside zigzags**: follow the stream. Or invent your own code, but make sure everyone knows what it means!

● Split into two teams. The trailblazers run ahead to lay a trail before lying in wait for the trackers. They must use plenty of arrows, particularly where several paths meet or where the route is overgrown.

● The trackers set off about ten minutes after the trailblazers. Once the trailblazers have been caught, the teams swap roles.

play the woodland mapping game

Make a three-dimensional map to find hidden treasure.

● Split into two or more teams. Each team chooses a small area of woodland, about the size of an average room, in which they hide treasure such as some chocolate coins.

● Each team makes a three-dimensional map of their area on a large piece of card or a tray or on the ground in a stick frame. Use twigs to represent trees, sticks and logs, and fix things together with clay if need be, to make a miniature version of the real woodland. Don't forget to mark where the treasure is!

● Using each other's maps, the teams try to find the treasure.

5

sunny sticks

52

make a sun clock

Use a stick to tell the time for a day and see how the earth moves in relation to the sun. Make sure you have a clock or a watch handy.

● Find an open area of ground that gets the sun all day – perhaps a beach (preferably above the high-tide line), a playground, a lawn or a patio. If you plan to keep your sun clock in that spot, make sure you use a place where it won't be disturbed.

● In the morning, push a straight 1m/3ft stick into the ground in the centre of the open area or, if you're using a site with a hard surface, place it in a plant pot. Make sure the stick is vertical.

● Every hour on the hour mark the tip of the stick's shadow with a short stick or a pebble, writing the number of the hour beside it if you wish!

● As, towards winter, the sun moves lower in the sky the shadows will change.

navigate with a stick

The sun rises in the east and sets in the west, and at midday in the northern hemisphere the sun is to the south. Armed with this knowledge, try using a stick as a compass.

● At midday, push a straight 1m/3ft stick into an open area of ground or sand where it casts a clear shadow. Mark the position of the shadow's tip with a pebble.

● Wait at least fifteen minutes and then mark the tip of the new shadow.

● Draw a straight line or place a stick through both marks: this is an approximate east–west line. If you stand on the line with the first mark (west) to your left and the second mark (east) to your right, you will be facing in a northerly direction. You can use a compass to check how accurate you are.

54

measure the earth

If you wanted to walk all the way around the world, how far do you think it would be? Back in the third century BC the Greek mathematician Eratosthenes worked out how to measure this – the Earth's circumference. The method described here is based on what he did (but of course he didn't have access to a mobile phone or a calculator!).

● Team up with some friends or a school as near as you can get to due north or south from you in the same time zone. Work out the distance between the teams (you can use the internet to help you with this).

● Each team should push a 1m/3ft stick vertically into the ground in an open, sunny spot, and then tie some string to the top. Make sure the top of each team's stick is exactly the same height above the ground.

● At midday, when the sun is at its highest, place the loose end of string at the end of each stick's shadow and secure it in place with a small stick, as illustrated.

● Using a protractor, measure the angle between the string and the top of the tall stick. Both teams must do this at exactly the same time– use a phone to keep in touch.

● Calculate the difference between the angle measurements at the two locations.

● To work out how far it is all the way around the Earth (its circumference, or C) use the following formula, where 360 refers to the fact that the Earth is a 360-degree sphere:

$$\frac{\text{Difference in angles}}{360} = \frac{\text{Distance between locations}}{C}$$

55

make shadow pictures

Can you conjure up shadows of magical creatures and scary monsters with a few sticks and leaves?

● You will need to find a place where the sun casts a shadow on a wall or the ground or some white card.

● Collect some interesting sticks. Push them into the ground and see what patterns their shadows make.

● Can you join the sticks together or attach leaves to make a funny stick person or a scary monster? Tear holes in leaves to make eyes or a mouth with fierce teeth.

● Can your friends guess what the shadow creatures are? Or can you put on a shadow puppet show?

6

musical sticks

56

make percussion sticks

There are lots of ways of using sticks to make a noise and beat a rhythm, such as dragging them along metal railings, hitting them together or playing percussion instruments such as this bottle xylophone.

● Choose two sturdy sticks about 40cm/16in long. Make sure you like the feel of them in your hands. The sticks will work perfectly well just as they are, but if you like you can peel off the bark, sand them for a nice smooth finish and decorate with natural paints (see page 6).

● Fill bottles with different amounts of water and some food colouring.

● Line the bottles up and play a tune. Can your friends name the tune?

make a stick rattle

This rattle is based on the sistrum, an African percussion instrument similar to a tambourine.

● Find things to rattle: perhaps broken shells or seed cases, or non-natural materials such as buttons, bottle tops or ring pulls.

● Choose a forked stick. Tie thin wire to the top of one of the forks, then thread some rattles along the wire. Twist the wire around the top of the other fork. If you want to make more noise you can tie lots of stick rattles together.

If you wish, decorate by stripping the bark off and painting it with natural paints, or make it into a story stick (see page 34).

58

bushcraft busking

This simple one-string guitar is based on an ancient design. You could experiment with different-sized cans and sticks – or even make your own guitar band.

● Find a tin can and a strong forked stick. Cut the two forks of the stick to the same length, at least twice the length of the can. Poke a hole through the bottom of the can with a bradawl.

● Thread strong, thin wire a little way through a button and twist it back on itself to secure the button. Thread the other end of the wire through the hole in the can and pull until the button lies flat against the can.

● Push the forks of the stick into the can until they touch the base. Pull the wire tight and tie it securely on to the stick just below the fork. The wire mustn't touch the stick until the point at which it is tied on.

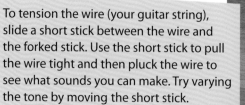

To tension the wire (your guitar string), slide a short stick between the wire and the forked stick. Use the short stick to pull the wire tight and then pluck the wire to see what sounds you can make. Try varying the tone by moving the short stick.

7

watery sticks

make a pond-dipping net ///

Use this net to discover water creatures from dragonflies and beetles to newts and shrimps.

● Cut off most of the legs from an old pair of tights, and then tie what is left with string to make a net.

● Bend a stick round to form a loop and secure with string. Wrap the waist of the tights around the loop a couple of times. Secure with a few stitches.

● Sweep the net through a pond or stream, then gently turn it inside out into a container of water. After looking at any creatures you catch, return them safely to where they came from.

play pooh sticks

///

Invented by Winnie-the-Pooh, this game is always fun to play on bridges crossing rivers or streams. On the count of three everyone drops their own clearly recognizable stick straight into the water from one side of the bridge, and then runs to the other side of the bridge to see whose stick appears first.

61

mini raft challenge

Try making some little rafts from natural materials. Perhaps they could carry stick people (see page 38) down a stream, across a puddle or a rock pool.

● Collect sticks of roughly equal length. Tie them together with creeper stems, raffia or string. The simplest designs work the best, but attaching a weight or keel directly underneath each boat will help keep them upright.

● Test how well your rafts float in some shallow water. If they are sturdy enough, line them up and let them go down a fast-flowing stream; the one that arrives first and intact at a prearranged spot downstream is the winner.

For a night-time treat, load each raft with a night light covered with the top section of a plastic bottle (to keep off the wind). Float the rafts on a garden pond for a magical effect; keep them tethered so that you can get them back safely.

62 make a fishing rod

● Cut a straight pole of living wood about 1.5–2m/5–6ft long. Cut a notch at the thinner end and then tie some line securely around the notch.

● Thread the line through a fishing hook and tie it securely with a good knot such as a blood knot. Bait the hook with an earthworm or some putty made from flour and water.

● Swing the line into the water, and then stand or sit very still. If the rod tip moves suddenly, you have a bite.

Fishing tips: Go out with an adult experienced in fishing. Only fish on watercourses where you have permission to fish. Handle fishing hooks with great care. When casting the rod, always check no one is near you.

measure the depth of a stream

How can you tell if a stream or a muddy puddle is too deep to cross? Use a long stick as a third leg to check!

● Put a long, sturdy stick next to your welly boot and place your finger at a point on the stick about 5cm/2in from the top of your boot. Now mark the stick at that point by carving a notch, drawing a line with a waterproof pen or tying a piece of grass around it.

● When crossing a stream or puddle, hold the stick vertically in the water ahead. If the water goes above the mark, look for a shallower place to cross (or take your boots off and wade in barefoot!).

If you come across a big muddy puddle, use a long stick to check if the gloopy mud will ooze over the top of your wellies.

8 woodcraft

and wildlife

make your own walking/tracking stick

Going for a walk is much more fun with a sturdy stick to help you along or a tracking stick to help you follow wild animals.

● Carefully cut a straight, sturdy green pole to a length you are comfortable with, probably about belly-button height. If you want a handle, choose a stick with a knobbly bit or a fork at one end. The stick must feel comfortable and strong but not heavy.

● Strip off the bark and then sand the wood for a smooth finish.

● Carve the bottom to a point. Harden the point by rotating it over a small fire for about five minutes. Carve the top if you wish.

● To use it for tracking, scratch lines at measured intervals and then roll some tight-fitting elastic bands along the stick. Use these to measure footprints and record stride length, so that you know where to look for the next print. For a professional job, glue a small button compass in the top (available from internet suppliers at low cost).

make a stretcher

Insert a couple of long, strong sticks through the body and arms of a zipped-up coat – very useful if any small people are getting tired! Perhaps you could pretend there has been an accident and practise basic first-aid techniques on each other; let's hope you never need to use them for real, but you should always be prepared.

make a mouse house

This neat little device is fun to make and might give you the chance to see a mouse close up. If you catch anything, just take a quick look at it before releasing it without handling it.

● Take two sticks of equal length, and two pieces of string. Tie the strings to each end of the sticks to make a square.

● Turn one stick round so that the string makes an X shape. Thread two slightly smaller sticks through the string so that they sit on top of the first sticks and at right angles to them. Keep threading pairs of progressively smaller sticks through in opposite directions as illustrated until you can't fit any more in. Weave green leaves or stems through for camouflage.

● Make a circle of bendy hazel or willow; attach it to one side of the trap with string. Place the house on the ground and push a forked twig upright into the earth in the centre of the circle.

● Place one end of a bendy twig on the bottom edge of the house through the forked stick. Lever the other end against the edge of the circle; the weight of the house bending the twig should hold the circle up off the ground. If an unsuspecting mouse steps on the circle, the house will fall over it.

● Place on an animal run and check regularly.

make a bug hotel

This creepy-crawly hotel provides shelter, food and a place to hibernate.

● Make a tube of chicken wire about 30cm/1ft long and 15cm/6in in diameter. Twist the wire ends round each other to secure.

● Push sticks through one end of the tube; this will be ground floor. Push more sticks and leaves down the tube, filling it completely. Put a flat piece of wood over the top so the hotel stays dry.

● Place the hotel in a sheltered spot in the garden, perhaps by a hedge or a tree. As material rots down, add more from the top.

make a habitat pile

A pile of sticks and leaves provides shelter and food for small creatures. Hedgehogs might hibernate, frogs seek shelter and creepy crawlies feed on the rotting wood. Choose a cool, shady, quiet spot and make a pile of leaves, sticks and logs. Check it occasionally to see who's living there, but always put the sticks back as you found them. Add new sticks as the old ones decay.

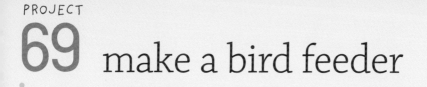

69 make a bird feeder

The simplest and best way to attract wildlife is just to feed the birds. You will be amazed by how close they come to feed.

● Mash some lard at room temperature and mix it with wild bird seed.

● Mould the mixture into a sausage shape and spread it over a dry branched stick with rough bark.

● Hang the stick from a tree or outside your window. The birds will perch on the little branches while tucking into their dinner.

● Keep a record of what birds you see and when the food's been eaten remember to add more.

plant a tree

If you plant a little stick tree with a few roots it will eventually grow into a huge tree providing shelter and food for wildlife, as well as lots of sticks for more games.

● Push a spade into the ground and wiggle it backwards and forwards to make a wedge-shaped hole.

● Gently twist the roots of a small tree until they are wound together in a bunch, and then place them gently into the prepared hole. Hold the tree and use your foot to push the soil down firmly all around the stem.

● To support and protect the tree, push a cane into the ground close to the stem, and then twist a rabbit guard around both tree and cane. Remove the cane and guard once the tree is established.

Water the tree in dry weather and remove any vigorous weeds. Keep an eye on your tree: how does it change with the seasons?

stick stuff

Have fun with sticks, but please follow these guidelines, which will help you to stay safe and look after the natural world:

General safety tips
- Never wield a stick or fire stick weapons at people or animals.
- Don't point sticks at people's faces.
- Take great care when running with sticks.
- When throwing sticks or things made from sticks, make sure everyone stays well out of the way.
- Watch out for splinters.
- Always take care when playing or exploring near water.
- Only use night lights or candles under adult supervision and never leave lanterns unattended.
- Don't collect poisonous berries or plants.
- Wash your hands after working with wild clay and other natural materials.

Fire safety guidelines
Always follow this basic safety guidance when using fire:
- Never make fire unless you have permission to do so and adults are around to supervise.
- Make fires well away from overhanging trees and buildings.
- Make fire on bare mineral soil, in a pit or (preferably) in a fire pan.
- Never light a fire in windy or excessively dry weather conditions.
- Never leave a fire unattended.
- Have a supply of water near by to extinguish the fire or soothe burns.
- Use as little wood as you can and let the fire burn down to ash. Once it is cold, remove all traces.

Tool safety guidelines
- Only use a knife or sharp tools if you have been given permission and shown how to use them safely.
- If using a knife, bradawl, skewer, secateurs or any other tool always have a first aid kit handy and make sure someone knows how to use it.

- Make sure everyone is aware of the potential dangers of using sharp tools. Accidents usually happen when people mess around.
- Think about where your blade is likely to go if it slips. Before using a knife, make sure there is an imaginary no-entry zone all around you. To check, stand up with your arms spread out and turn around; you shouldn't be able to touch anyone or anything.
- Never cut over your lap – the femoral artery in the thigh carries large volumes of blood and if it is severed you will lose a pint of blood a minute.
- Work the blade away from your body, and away from the hand supporting the wood. Never cut towards your hand until you can use a knife with great control.
- Always cut on to a firm surface such as a steady log.
- If you need to pass a knife to someone else, always do so with the handle pointing towards the other person.
- Always put tools away when they are not in use; never leave them lying around.
- Knives should only be used when you are participating in craft activities. A knife is a tool and never a weapon.
- Give knives and other sharp tools the respect they deserve: always stick to the rules.

Leaving no trace
All the activities in this book should be carried out with respect for the natural world.
- Respect all wildlife.
- Be considerate to other users of the countryside.
- Take all litter home with you.
- Take responsibility for your own actions.
- Only collect loose plant materials that are common and in abundance; don't over-collect sticks.
- Leave wild places as you find them.

Other information
Suppliers of willow withies: www.willowwithies.co.uk and www.windrushwillow.com
Suppliers of wet-strength tissue: www.musgrovewillows.co.uk and www.economyofbrighton.co.uk

index

acknowledgments

Many thanks to the following for help and advice: Julia Donaldson, Michael and Claire Morpurgo (www.farms4citychildren.co.uk); Jane and Bob White; Jeremy Hastings (Islay Birding); Chris Holland and Chris Salisbury (Wildwise); Roger Harrington (www.bisonbushcraft.co.uk); Jon-Paul Lamoureux; Martin Burkinshaw; Lynnie Donkin; Joe O'Leary (www.wilderness-survival.co.uk) and everyone else who shared ideas with us at the Wilderness Gathering; Sean O'Leary; Anita Osborne; Ben Haydon; Hereward Corbett; David Gosling; David Millin; Jenny Hanwell; Gordon MacLellan (working as Creeping Toad); Robin Hull; Malcolm Appleby; James and Helen Jackson; Nigel Adams; Kate Cheng; Iain Naismith; Ollie Rathmill; Chris Parker; Polly Scott and her reception class; Caroline, Colin, Clifford, Frankie and Anya Carr; and the many other families and friends who have supported us in so many ways.

A big thank-you to all the young people who took part in activities: Raymond C and brothers, Bluebell R and Will A; Tom U; Jonathon and Jessie A; Lily, Charlie and Toby R; Agnes K; Carolyn S; Clifford, Frankie and Anya C; Anna, Tim, Nicholas and Ella V; Alice and Jonny F; Fiona and Eliza N; Freddy L; Tilly S; Lucas R; Rebecca and Edward W; Alexander B; Matt, Tris and Will E; Natasha and Adam H; Anna, Laura and Ben W; Sophie T; Isabella G; Catherine F; Milly B; Tilly G; Rebecca M; Lydia, Helena and Lucian S; David C; Milly H; Christopher and Sienna W; Scott H; Ama and Mahalia J; Danny, Jess and Natali K; Kate W; Tsering L; Ella W; Jess R; Imogen B; Hannah M; Sarah P; Ellen B; Rose P; Kerry W; Libby and George W; Lucy B; Hamish, Isobel and Oliver M; Alexander and Mimi D; Magnus G; Josh G; Milissa D; Yanni K; Sam B; Tallula, Noah and Poppy C; Scarlet R; Carla, Louie, Stan and Frankie C; Holly P; Sam V; Ayrton K; Daisy and Monty S; Amy, Annabel and Matilda S; Megan S; Scott M; Sophie and Elli B; Daniel W.

Many thanks to our husbands, Ben and Peter, and our children, Jake, Dan, Connie, Hannah and Edward, for their support and all the fun outdoor adventures we have shared over the years.

And finally, thanks to everyone at Frances Lincoln.